LIKE THAT

LIKE THAT

MATTHEW YEAGER

FORKLIFT_BOOKS

FORKLIFT BOOKS EDITION, MARCH 2016

ISBN 978-0-9903082-6-3

Edited by Matt Hart

Book and cover design by Eric Appleby

Cover & author photos by Mateusz Broughton

For a complete listing of titles, please visit

WWW.FORKLIFTBOOKS.COM

For more on this book, visit

WWW.H-NGM-N.COM/LIKETHAT

AN IMPRINT OF

for Jerry Rippey

"...[THE ATTEMPT] TO SAY MATTER IN TERMS
OF SPIRIT, OR SPIRIT IN TERMS OF MATTER,
TO MAKE THE FINAL UNITY. THAT IS THE
GREATEST ATTEMPT THAT EVER FAILED. WE
STOP SHORT JUST THERE."

—ROBERT FROST

CONTENTS

LIKE THAT

A Big Ball of Foil in a Small NY Apartment

"IT WILL FLAME OUT..."

—HOPKINS

It began with a single sheet, leftover from his lunch.

His unthinking palm had reached out to it, slapped down

on the center of it, and begun gathering and compacting

until soon he had a small firm ball in his fist.

He squeezed the ball tightly, as tightly as he could.

Now the ball was, if not as firm as possible,

at least as firm as he could easily make it,

and he took from this the small satisfaction it offered.

It felt good. In fact, as his fingers opened out

into their individual selves again, and he saw the ball

resting in his slightly red, dented palm, as in a nest,

it occurred to him that there were many good things

to be felt about this ball: its crinkled surface

would keep it from rolling off at the slightest tilt;

it wouldn't come undone on it own as balled-up paper can;

and that it was all crumpled foil, 100% through

seemed to contain a kind of meaning,

(though truly what it was he wasn't sure)....

It was then that he had an idea. Like light on water

it danced across his thinking, absorbing his attention.

He would add to this ball, add to it until it was huge!

He wouldn't throw it out as he had so many others.

And how many had he thrown out? The unknowable number

(exaggerated for effect) jostled him all over, like nerves,

for you see, he had already begun to imagine the ball quite large,

and the thought that the foil in his little ball

might have existed as a nearly flat sheet on the surface

of an already enormous ball boggled him.

(But he knew it wasn't good to think like that,

and he snapped quickly to, nodding and determined.)

He would grow the ball from this point forward.

Foil was everywhere. It wouldn't be hard.

So from that day on as he walked the streets,

although he let his thoughts drift as they wished,

(seeing, for instance, the sun seep free from behind a cloud

he'd think, in the brief spell before it disappeared behind another,

of hundreds of suddenly pleased sunbathers in rows on a beach;

4

he'd think of sweaty red-faced men carrying heavy wooden crates)

he kept his sights always alive to the prospect

of foil's particular glint. When he'd see a stranded sheet

in a corner garbage can or on a restaurant table,

he'd glance sharply about, to see if anyone was watching him,

slyly pocket it, then shuffle off at a quickened pace.

Early on, it bothered him, and he'd have to reassure himself:

"No one is looking; no one cares; this city is full

of stranger things than a man collecting foil."

Over time, he began to believe this truth, or rather,

the shame he couldn't help but feel was overcome.

For there was nothing much better than walking about,

as twilight approached, with a good take bulging his pockets.

It was a feeling not unlike knowing a wonderful secret,

or being, perhaps, a bottle with a message in it.

However, at such bright excited times,

much like an island surfacing in a drought-sucked stream,

the ball as he wished it could be, huge and shining

and exactly round, would give rise in his mind.

It was awesome and beautiful, but not a good thing,

and he tried to keep it from happening, to hide it away,

like that heart under the floorboards in the Poe story

that had so terrified him as a child. For his own ball

when he'd return home, became so inadequate then,

so silly and lopsided and small. Emptying his pockets,

smoothing the foil with a rolling pin (his system),

he'd murmur sound, sobering sayings to himself like:

"nothing turns out the way you thought it would,"

and "it'll take years." But time was one thing he had,

and his progress, albeit slow (as each added scrap was a smaller

and smaller piece of the growing whole) was steady.

As the months went by, the ball grew. It grew and grew.

It grew until it had to be moved from the oven,

where he'd kept it to save space, into the open, onto the floor.

It grew till it couldn't fit through the window or the door.

It grew until furniture had to be moved, first

to new places in his apartment, then out onto the street.

It was then he knew the ball was there to stay....

But though he'd been the one that had wanted the ball,

though he'd been the one that had built the ball,

often he felt ambivalently, and this ambivalence grew too.

Why was he doing what he was?

Why was he filling his apartment, his mind, with foil?

It was not something he preferred to wonder about,

and he tried hard to keep the wondering out, to ignore it

as one might a dog that's scratching at a door....

But ridiculous as he acknowledged the ball to be,

if you were to have caught him at the right moment,

you would have seen how he loved it.

Certain nights, after he'd measured it in all directions

(by setting up a spotlight and measuring the shadows)

then peeled and patched it to preserve its roundness,

(the ball's defining, so most important quality)
he'd step away (as away as he still could),
and those narrowed-up, fault-inventing eyes of his
would soften into something like appreciation.
Spotlit like that, the ball gave back a cool, fragile light
much as he heard the earth did when seen by astronauts,
and he'd feel suddenly lucky to be where he was,
standing in such strange and silvery shine. Coming to,
he'd often find an inch of ash on his cigarette....
So it was kind of sad then, that his ball should end,
should stop growing, even though all along
it'd been what he'd been working toward.
Would he still see a city speckled with foil?
Or would what once was treasure dull
to trash again? There was no way to predict.
The night he was done, the night the ball
nudged up against his ceiling and his walls
(a coincidence so long foreseen it had lost its luster)
he pressed his teeth deep into its surface,
as a kind of unreadable signature,
leaned his confused body against it, closed his eyes,
and, listening to the cars pass, wept a little bit.

—SEPTEMBER, 2003

7

Tap Water

When a woman enters your life you can either
change or not change and by "not change" I do
not mean "remain the same" because that would be
impossible. Say it turns out she doesn't drink
tap water. What do you do? You either stop drinking
tap water or you begin emphatically drinking
tap water. "I love tap water," you say. "Its faint
metallic odor stirs up all sorts of pleasant memories
in me of summer camp, greenish pool water
trails at twilight, fireflies" Of course you have
no idea if this is true, but look, she is laughing,
she's laughing in a way that says, "tell me more," so
you do, out of your mouth comes an impromptu

treatise on the virtues of tap water, and like that,

without intending it, you've become a committed drinker

of tap water. It is no price to pay for charming her.

And so down streets you two stroll, she

with her bottle of water, you with one of her old

bottles of water filled back up with plain old

tap water. Months pass, this scene repeats, there are

leaves on the sidewalks then snow on the sidewalks

then leaves again. And each time she fills

back up a bottle with tap water for you and you

tip it to your lips, squeezing the wrinkled plastic

a little it's like an additional puff of air blown

on something drying; soon you're set. "Just

give him tap water," she says to a waiter,

"he likes it." And probably you do like it.

At very least you enjoy the joy she gets out of it,

this perceived eccentricity; it is larger, more important,

I mean, than the almost undetectable difference

between bottled water and tap. And truthfully

the tap water is a nice example of the way small things

become large in your life. Over time what sprung

from near-nothing, from your delight at her delight

at something you just blurted has become a large

and important component of who it is you are to her.

And who you are to her has become, of course,

an important component of who you are to you.
She says to you one night, "Remember
when you told me two years ago you liked to drink
tap water? Well, I opened my mouth in the shower
the next morning and drank some." And maybe
it's here you become aware that this influencing
business has been, the entire time, going both ways.
And what a crazy moment this is. One tends to think
for no reason that influence is a one-way street, and that
the steady stream flows only toward you. But would she
have opened her mouth in the shower were it not
for you? Would she brush her teeth with shower water
(as you know her to do)? You feel alive as you do
when you pinch yourself. You notice it more. She remarks
she loves the almost visible smells of Chinatown
in late spring when the new heat has loosened and freed
the cold-sealed odors of street trash and the sun has warmed
the inch of brown water in the bottoms of the garbage cans.
"It's like you and your tap water," she says. "It smells,
but I love the memories it uncurls."
And so on and so on and so on.... Now, for the heck of it,
let us row back up this series of happenings,
to where this set-in-its-ways river that is the case
of tap water thins to a ribbon re-routable with the edge
of a hand. To the source I mean. Say that first time

you set two glasses of tap water on the counter, and she

said to you that, no, sorry, she didn't drink

tap water, you asked her, "Why?" Say you then listened

to a litany of reasons (perhaps a horrifying news story)

and also kept listening as she recalled

specific instances in which she's remained thirsty

because of her steadfast refusal. Say right then

and there you loudly give up drinking

tap water. You purchase, the very next day, a sink filter,

which might as well be a present, as you've bought it

for her. And she sees the filter, and she likes it;

she says "when did you get this? You didn't tell me

you got this" and a sort of light

is thrown on you. Now, instead of being someone

that prefers un-preferable aspects of life for odd reasons,

you are in her eyes someone who is willing to change.

You are flexible as un-frozen water! Time, of course,

continues to move in this version of the story as well.

Leaves, snow, and petals cycle in with the sidewalk trash;

small items change apartments; you see all each others'

clothes. However, you wave a hand say sorry I don't drink

tap water anymore to your buddy as he sets two glasses

on the counter. "Really?" he says, "You stopped drinking

tap water? When did that happen?" to which you say,

"Some time ago." "And you know," you say to her as she pours

bottled water for two over big ice cubes at some restaurant,
"I think I'm feeling better since I've quit drinking
tap water. Seriously I want to thank you I'm breathing
easier, sleeping longer, sleeping deeper all because
of you." And the truth is, you are feeling better. Perhaps
it has to do more with her mere presence, the fact of her
whole being putting out warmth behind your
sleeping shoulders, but who cares what you chalk it up to?
Now, this is not to say that doubt doesn't figure in.
Say home alone one night you end up sticking a glass
under the bathroom faucet, pour yourself a tap water
wait as it turns from gray to clear, take a drink
and wonder, "What is wrong with this? What is wrong
with the way I used to be? Perhaps you look around your
bathroom and wonder what it is you'd have been thinking
right then were you not thinking about, of all things
tap water? You exist; your bathroom exists; there is
a decent enough chance, you'd be there,
barefoot on its tiles, that very moment, thinking some
thought or other. One could, of course, say this
about any moment, any situation, and therefore feel
a sense of astonishment at the bizarre and circumstantial
choices, whims, accidents, etc. that have ping-ponged you
into the particular mental situation you presently are in....
You could say it as certainly as you say you are

older than you are in any of your photographs,

but it is really better not to think like that,

not to keep obsessively polishing to a shine the dimes

on which your very real life has turned

Regrets can come from that. You feel blessed

but you also feel regrets. And drinking only

tap water or not drinking tap water at all from one

single point forward is just one example. It is one leaf

on a tree of leaves that change naturally from green

to another color when a woman enters your life.

You find yourself turning sharply into different

types of stores, stores where the clerks give you

looks, making mental notes, almost or actually

purchasing flowers, and your life continues as such.

So what happens to you, though, you who have either

stopped drinking tap water or begun

emphatically and only drinking tap water? Well,

chances are your relationship begins to come apart

at a certain point because that is simply what happens

to most relationships. Blame it on circumstance, time, timing,

change or nothing changing. Suddenly there's a crack,

and the crack widens into a blackness wide as night.

She shifts in your perspective from someone

who simply does not drink tap water into

"one of those people who doesn't drink tap water"

which means she is too good for things that are fine
for everyone else. Can any detail serve as a stand-in
for a whole person? "This is everything that is wrong
with you," she says one evening. "What?" you ask.
"You have handed me these scissors wrong," she says.
 "If you loved me you would offer me the handles!"
"What?" you repeat. "I just forgot," you say,
"I was thinking about something." But now you are one
that thinks so much about matters other
than his love that he could actually do such a thing,
could actually hand her scissors wrong, and maybe
as the door closes and you take your hand off the knob
and stand a moment in some florescent hallway,
you realize, sadly, that she has a point....
When a woman has entered your life and then
left it you are changed and while you may change
forward into something resembling what you once were
you most certainly do not change back. That
is impossible. Soon she is a memory and comes to mind
when you see, say, hair worn the way she used to wear her hair,
or meet someone with her same first name, or see
the breed of dog she liked, or find yourself
by yourself on a certain block. And certainly
you do think of her at least some of the time
when you loosen a faucet and have a drink

of tap water, or when you meet someone that feels

a particular way about the stuff. But then again, perhaps

you don't split, what do I know? Perhaps the crack

is put into perspective, which is to say, understood

made small. I don't understand how it is possible,

but there is plenty of evidence, for better or for worse,

hell, I am a product of it, that all love does not end

with long voicemail messages, gulping, then moving on.

—JULY, 2005

Sleep, Mothers

It is two it is three it is four in the morning

They are sleeping think of them sleeping

It is two it is three it is four in the morning

All in their beds think of them, think of them sleeping

The gray-haired mothers are sleeping

Out walking, walking home, you are still out walking

Like houses viewed from incoming airplanes—tiny and so

       many—

The gray-haired mothers are sleeping

You have this thought, it comes to you out of night, out of the

       hour on your watch,

out of the motion of your feet, out of the emptied sidewalk

An organization of nerves

you think of them, think of them sleeping

Warm in warm rooms under covers to their chins

they are sleeping, the gray-haired mothers are sleeping

Their eyelids are shut their faces are washed their bangs are

        bobby-pinned

In nightgowns they pull from boxes at Christmas

In nightgowns chosen from department store sale racks

(and the clicking sound of hangers on sale racks)

You think of them, think of them sleeping

It is 1:56 it is 2:28 it is 3:07 exactly in the morning

In big houses in small houses in dream houses in apartments

In houses where the furniture will no longer be rearranged

They are sleeping the gray-haired mothers are sleeping

In single beds in double beds in queen and king sized beds

In beds that they remake each morning

On couches in hospital beds in beds they've owned

for twenty years or more they are sleeping

Like dolls inside dollhouses as little girls they played with dolls

and if they could see that childhood dollhouse now....

Their eyelids are shut they are sleeping

Their husbands are snoring

Next to them snoring down the hall behind closed doors

snoring in another city snoring

On the hall clocks on the kitchen clocks

on the clocks on their nightstands large in red numbers silent

on the watches taken off and placed on the nightstands

on the special occasion watch in the jewelry box
on the inherited clock in a small house's nicest room
on the microwave clock visible from the table
where the husband in a white undershirt smokes cigarettes
and laughs to himself remembering football
In the wooden chair he always sits in he can hardly walk

It is two it is four it is three in the morning
Think of their glasses on nightstands they are folded
Think of their books on nightstands they are quiet and shut
Think of their phones they are quiet unringing
We think of them we think of them we think of them
They come to us, they whirl as loose nightgowns
in the night air above us it is like a Chagall
Night after night counting street signs
Night after night counting street signs
Hands in my pockets hands clutching backpack straps hands
frightened into fists one around a ridiculous little knife
the sound of my feet the exact speed I am walking
From pool of streetlight to pool of streetlight
I think of them sleeping, I think of them sleeping,
Light-switches smudged from much touching are off
Electric bulbs in their sockets are cool to the touch
Only the refrigerator is running
a hum somewhere she is not hearing
And the room I visualize is mine

And the room you visualize is yours personal

And you wonder, where has it gone

That bed down the hall behind the door with the loose glass knob

That bed twice the size of yours containing all those pillows

        one pillow for you

And you wonder where has she gone

She would put her palm on your forehead

Surely it has only shifted form

Surely she is somewhere

Down some figurative hall behind some figurative door

        behind some figurative glass knob

They are sleeping, they are sleeping, they are sleeping

Their breathing is soft it is hard to hear as rain

is to see out a window at night when it's mid-air

It is one it is two it is three in the morning

They don't know one another they are one another

Would your mother and my mother be friends?

They would all be friends they are alike as taxis

they want the phone to ring on Sunday and it be their child,

their child who is always their child

Inside them their plans for tomorrow are sleeping

Inside them their love for their children is sleeping

Inside them the names of so many they know are sleeping

Their names are Jan and Joanne and Marcy-Ann and Mary Jo

Their names are Margaret and Harriet and Nancy

Their names are Kathy and Janet and Diana and Debbie
Names they've had their lives entire
Someone has died someone will die
They will ring doorbells holding food in casserole dishes
Someone has died someone will die
Prayer cards will be pressed by magnets to refrigerators
(And the unchanging magnets on their refrigerators)
Someone has died someone will die
They will take their husbands to doctors
They will sit in waiting rooms patient and waiting
They will sit in waiting rooms with ferns and read magazines
They will write checks, they will wait they will rise they will sleep
They are sleeping, the gray-haired mothers are sleeping
They are breathing
Their children have left them, it is sad but not like it was
On such occasions we say that is life
Their children have left and live in cities and are busy they
        know that
Someone is dying and someone will die
On such occasions we say that is life
Their children have left and call, when they call, on Sundays
On their nightstands there are lamps
they can turn on in the dark like blind women feeling with
        their fingers
On their nightstands there are rosary beads
and in a frame leaning back in some photo

children who will always be children because always they are

      mothers,

children who have left and call, when they call, on Sundays

It is one it is two it is three in the morning

Think of them sleeping, think of their sleep.

              —SUMMER, 2009

Poem

You're Henry Hudson;

the month is June, the year is 1611, the time of day

still very early in the morning;

you're wearing Henry Hudson's gray, linsey-woolsey 17th

        century pajamas

you're breathing through Henry Hudson's nose

you're Henry Hudson, and at this moment you are cold, quite

        cold,

your fingers especially, and your ears.

But alas, you can't throw another log on the fire

because you aren't in a bed in England.

Nor are you in Holland in an inn.

Nor are you in your ship's cabin.

You're in a lifeboat, Henry, an open-air shallop,

in the middle of an icy bay north of Canada

with your hands tied behind your back, bobbing.

The sea is blue.

The sea is dark as blue can be while still being absolutely blue.

The sky is blue, is a different kind of blue.

The cold is blue, a third blue, a feeling.

And you're Henry Hudson, and one hour ago, you were asleep;

you were in your bunk in your cabin on your back,

you were rocking, there was weird northern purple

slipping through your porthole, all was good.

Now you are watching your own ship sail away without you on it.

You're Henry Hudson,

and you are having a hard time believing it.

When your crew knocked down your door,

when they dragged you from your cabin,

when they put a pistol to your forehead,

when they bound your wrists and lowered you into the boat,

you don't know,

DREAM, was your knee-jerk reaction.

Then, when events revealed themselves to be

too linear, too continuous to be a dream, you thought: BLUFF.

You didn't think they had it in them.

You're Henry Hudson. No one among them

is Henry Hudson. No one among them is even close.

And when they cut the rope, setting you loose,

you were still running ration numbers in your head:

"What kind of an increase could I logically afford
to give these guys to win back their affections?"
And when they set sail, when the sails popped full,
when the ship began to progress into a speck,
you thought, "Another minute and they'll turn around."
You said to yourself, "Be patient, Henry.
They'll realize they're lost without you,
They'll throw you a line, tow you through the cold,
teach you a lesson. And even if you aren't humbled,
you'll pretend to be humbled. For them. Out of love."

You're Henry Hudson; you have not moved,
except up and down, slightly, nonstop;
your shrinking ship has by now disappeared from view.
It is later, brighter, worse; you aren't alone.
Your son is with you, and the ship's sick and dying.
You're Henry Hudson, so naturally these other men
look at you; they have watched you, watched you
watching the ship then the speck then the blank sky and sea.
They believe not their own eyes, but yours.
They believe not their own hearts, but yours.
They interpret your every mumble, your every eyebrow twitch.
Here we are, in the era where self-mastery,
among virtues, reigns supreme. Here we are.
You are on a shallop with no oars, no mast, no sails, no rigging,
no way of moving through water

save everyone's cupped hands. It is neither

a bluff nor a dream. You see, out there,

in the bright morning, your end;

it is sky and ice and sun and water;

and there sure is a lot of water beneath you, Henry,

(and you feel that in a shallop, boy do you,

so much more in a shallop than in a ship).

You are in what may or may not be an impossible situation.

There is nothing on the shallop to eat

except people; don't go there, Henry. First,

the inhumanity of it all. The injustice of it all.

One minute you're in bed.

One minute you're one season away

from sailing through the Northwest Passage.

Now you're marooned so far north of shit-fuck-anywhere

your long-game is freezing to death in June.

It is insane to you. June.

But if there's a person alive that can find his way back, it is you.

You're the greatest explorer in the world.

Tell yourself that, Henry, in a steady voice; it's not a lie.

It's not even the slightest exaggeration.

In the direst circumstances, you surprise yourself.

You make one surprising, correct decision after another.

That is who you are, what you do.

And you want people to know this.

You want people to know that back in 1609,

you were hired to find a water route to China;

the vision of your Dutch financiers

was to sail east, over the top of Russia.

Of course you'd already tried this.

You told them as much; you said, "As impossibilities go

sailing over the top of Russia very, very impossible."

They said, "Henry, sail to China over the top of Russia,"

and you said, "OK then," and shook their hands,

and once past their horizon, you said,

"Fuck this nonsense; I'm Henry Hudson," turned abruptly left,

sailed west, sailed, kept sailing, kept the faith, sailed over a month,

saw birds, hit land, followed a wooded coastline,

found an unexpected opening, came up into an incredible

            natural harbor,

a slender island of solid rock, a wide blue river,

sailed up this river as far as you could, past trees, 100 ft evergreens,

encountered natives with no idea whatsoever

they were dressed like European kings,

in sable, in martin, in black fox, in silver fox, in bear, in beaver;

"Oh, and by the way," you said to your financiers,

"these natives will GIVE US these furs

for fishing hooks, worn out knives, dinged kettles, pieces of

            cloth, pocket mirrors,

and they will not believe their luck

at having encountered such idiots as us!"

And your financiers forgave you, Henry.

They more than forgave you; they rejoiced at you!

They smacked you on the back and the butt.

They said, "Great job, Henry. You amaze us. God bless you!"

You're Henry Hudson, and you want to be forgiven like that.

You're Henry Hudson, and you are used to being forgiven like that.

You are used to deserving forgiveness.

You're Henry Hudson and you've made one mistake, as you see it.

Only one real mistake. And in such a life!

Amidst such a tremendous volume of decisions!

You went too far north too late in the season.

The year was 1610; oh you were back in the Americas already,

only a year later; you were farther north,

and you weren't just poking around this time.

You had the Northwest Passage clear in your sights;

only land could stop your seeing it,

and land was nowhere in sight; you were sailing

through an oceanic bay, all day, every day;

the water just kept spreading, and it was your experience, Henry.

You were off the edge of all maps;

you were on a globe in your own head,

but unfortunately on this globe in your own head,

all the known land masses were draped

over a slightly underestimated ball, yes,

working, as you undeniably were, (and still are),

with this smaller, older, lesser-known,

much less watery planet earth firmly, very firmly,

in your 17th century mind, your plan was to curve

as far left toward China as you could get

while still getting back to Labrador by October.

It was a fine plan. Everyone agreed.

But you just sailed out a few days too far.

You damned dummy, Henry, you sailed too far toward China.

You did, and on your way back, the ice

started reaching all around you, starting coming

out of the sea to surround you.

You got stuck, Henry, and others with you.

Was it entirely your fault? Yes, yes it was.

Did you admit it? Yes, yes you did,

and the men, the men didn't like it, but what could they do?

And you, you didn't like it either, but you're Henry Hudson,

so you did what you could;

you ate rations; you sat in your cabin;

you wrote in your log; you read both your books;

you looked out your porthole;

you occasionally addressed your men as a whole,

and they seemed fine to you, maybe a little annoyed,

a little haggard, noses a little crusty, but fine, tough,

not Henry Hudson tough, but tough, men,

men that understood that as soon as the ice thawed

and cracked the greatest explorer in the world

would guide them all the way to China....

And this, amazingly, was so few months ago

that it was weeks ago, and now, somehow,

you are undeniably standing on a shallop

in the middle of this cold, cold bay!

You are standing on a shallop being gaped at

by your son and the sick and the dying,

and they are waiting for you to tell them what to do,

and you still don't know what to do.

You're Henry Hudson, and what you'd like to know

is where your warning was! Seriously, where was it?

Did they even try to warn you?

Well, then they should have tried harder.

They should have said, "Listen, we're not Henry Hudsons;

we're weak, we're afraid, we're not very smart."

They should have spoken their guts.

You're actually a very good listener.

Instead, you make one mistake, they hold their feelings in,

      and they mutiny!

You have made ONE MISTAKE DAMMIT!!!!

CAN THIS BE WHAT YOU GET?!!!

      And the sea, if the sea could speak, would say,

      I I I. Me Me Me. I am the sea, and I am the same,

      mostly, as I'll always be, not for you to drink

or breathe, freakier than you can bear to think,

and you will sink inside me, Henry,

into me, you and the deeds you did atop me

in your measly crumb of a ship; they'll sink with you,

with your puny body, its eentsy skeleton,

and your name will shoot out as dye

cannot quite inside me; your name will shoot out

like holiness in a drop of holy water added

to a larger body of unholy water,

though you are not holy, not holy at all, to me.

And I, an unholy body of water the size of Europe,

an unnamed Eden of a freezing sea,

will nonetheless take on your surname, Henry,

and wear it for awhile, like a skin,

before I cast it off. Because I like you, Henry.

You make me laugh! You're a funny little guy,

fuming in a little boat, wondering what you get,

not seeing that you are, in fact, what I get.

See, there are creatures deep down in me

that will find you worth eating, creatures

whose blood is telling them they would rather eat you

than cease being, and they are my children

and breathe my salty water and know it as my love.

You're Henry Hudson;

you're Henry mother-fucking Hudson;

it's not that you do not admit defeat easily,

it's that you don't admit defeat! Who, pray tell,

is the Ponce de Leon of the Northern Sea, if not you?

You're Henry Hudson and, yes, even at this moment,

a Northwest Passage! You can have the dream.

Oh, and it is good; it is still so, so good;

you can have the dream, Henry,

of passing through the Northwest Passage

and knowing it, of the unending light of northern summer,

of shimmering cliffs of ice in a continuous sun,

of the seals honking and slapping something like applause.

You can see yourself putting in

at Dartmouth, England, bony, bearded, quiet.

Then you put the tea on the table. Bam.

You put the furs on the table. Bam.

You put the china on the table. Delicately.

You put so much gold on the table

the table bows! Then, as piece de resistance

you lay the Northwest Passage itself on the table;

a wiggle of ink. Ah!

Guess what, world? It exists, and I have found it!

There is a way through, and I have felt it!

That's what you say....

You're Henry Hudson, and you see clearly now,

larger than ever, your end; you can no longer

not see it for more than a moment;

it is sky and ice and water; it is the yellow and blue

skin and chattering teeth of the sick and dying.

Like an idiot you are chuckling, giggling, laughing.

Like a sick man you are chuckling, giggling, shaking your

        head, your finger.

Once, you were a helluva cabin boy, Henry.

Now you are where you are, on a boat

with no oars, no masts, no sails, no rigging,

no means of harnessing wind, no means of moving through water.

You're the greatest explorer of your moment,

and that is not going to matter much longer.

No, that is going to matter forever.

Among the sick and dying and your son, you're the obvious leader.

And once you are freed (because your mutinous crew,

before it sailed away, tossed a knife into the boat,

just to make things interesting), yes, once you are freed,

you look the shivering, terrified men over.

You tuck the knife into your belt, and you see.

Nature is about to perform her quick work.

You will lead them all, with grim solemnity, into the sea....

No, you think, I'm Henry Hudson,

and the last one I eat will be my son.

Red Wine or White Wine

Wed wine. Wood wine. What wine. Wet wine.

Read that first line again iambically,

and that's what it sounds like coming out

guests' mouths in the din of each and every

catered New York cocktail party:

"awouldWINE, please?" Sometimes

I ask for clarification; mostly I just guess;

it's like betting colors in roulette; that's a lie;

I never just guess; I'm conscientious;

you lock me in a closet and pay me to guard

the darkness, the hangers, the rod,

I'll figure out how; I'll finger each hanger

individually; no sir, I only turn, reach,

and pluck up a stem glass when I distinctly

hear or mis-hear the "red" or "white"

someone must want in the "wet,"

"wood," "what," "wed." Sometimes a man

will order "awhridWHINE?"

three, four times in a row, right at my ear;

like a golfer botching one short putt

after another, overcompensating "uh-wreh-

TWINE? Wreght-TWIDE," he'll grow baffled,

then louder, into the pitch of anger,

then direct that anger at me, the bartender,

as if my ear was some trick hole

that moved, or coughed out balls.

But I'm not an asshole.

("I'm a poet, sir; and poets' ears are like

golf ball washers; in them words dirty from use

come clean like scrubbed little moons.")

What I am is a catering bartender.

That's what the mirror tells me;

that's what the tax stubs tell me;

that's what a closet half-composed

of near-disposable button-down shirts,

(which I don't dispose of, ever,

but bleach whiter, RIT-dye blacker)

has said at each opening for a decade....

Whatever it is you are, does it really matter?

That's what I ask but have no answer.

I do anything like I do everything,

for better or worse, with all my pride.

I've poured, on average, 2000 glasses of wine

a week for actually eleven years now;

As Tennyson learned melancholy,

through practice, I've learned so much

about high volume pouring it could be said,

by comparison, that I know nothing

about anything else. What I've found?

That there are laws with wine, as in planes

and crashes, laws of accident, averages.

If you work with wine, wine will collect:

on your cuffs in stippled little drops,

where your shirt puffs, as facts in your head,

under your sink, in the bathroom mirror,

3 am, on your tongue, red; no matter

how many times you pour, no matter

the smoothness of your wrist, it will drip.

Due to bottle-lip shape, due to fins

of miscut foil messing up the final

lift-then-twist, it will always sometimes drip,

and when a dropped crimson tear

smacks linen, bleeds, someone very rich

looks at you for one second.

You wish they wouldn't.

You wish they wouldn't look at you at all.

And the looks have added up into

a permanent line in my forehead, a mouth

shaped somewhat like that line.

Every mistake I've ever made

with wine I've made at least twice.

And sometimes what a guest has said

sounds enough to me like "white" or "red"

that I pick up a glass, pour, end up

trying to hand over red for white, white for red.

Even if it's the fault of people

who spin around to their Blackberries

before confirming, or who, in the name

of manners don't match their volume

to the volume of the room, or whose tongues

are already sticky and thick, still

out goes my voice in its best cheery shit drawl.

"My, goodness, sir! I am so so sorry!"

And I shake my head once, and hard,

as if such a thing has happened to others,

but never before that moment to me.

But I tell the truth there. I am sorry.

Sorry as a sore on a tongue.

I am sorry that this has happened,

that it has happened, in fact, again.

My job, here at this moment, consists

of matching a word with a color,

and there are, at a typical cocktail party,

only two options, capable of being

simplified into red and white;

forgive me my repetition, amplification.

My job here consists of

matching a word with a color.

How do you think people look at you

when you fail at that?

Like you're great?.... Let's deflect the locus.

Let's hang on a bit with one another.

You know the situation that ensues

when a question begins "Do you mind?"

—as in "Do you mind if I borrow a swipe

of your deodorant?"—how the reply, "No,"

might mean no or yes depending?

And the situation that ensues when, driving a car,

you say, "and then I take a left?"

and someone says, "right," instead of "correct?"

The similarity in the palate stopped "d"

in red and the palate-stopped "t" in white

is like those, and it is real and it is an

inescapable part of a life I've chosen.

Night after night after night.

Amidst the music of a party,

amidst the cacophonic clapping sounds

of partygoers' talk (like a flock of meat-eating birds

they squawk beneath the music),

the English language fails; it fails at its job;

it fails to properly divide;

if the word for "red" was "shack" and the word

for "white" was just a long "eeeeee" sound,

like a nasal bottle rocket fired parallel

to the ground "Eeeeeeeeeeeeeeeeeeee! Wine!

my life might be grand; you don't know;

this alone might make my life grand.

Maybe my life is that close; spiffed up in a tux,

one night at the Top of the Rock,

the next at Gotham Hall, listening to quality

live jazz, working quick, in rhythm,

with my hands. "I would like one shack

wine and one eeeeeeeee wine;" there's no chance

anyone would ever get two glasses

the same color. No chance! I'd get it right

every time. There'd be a kind of honor,

There'd be less dishonor, a cool plateau....

Because it's a special look I get from the men,

mid 3os, my own age now, risers in their fields,

when they try to order awidtWINE,

and I pour them out a wine

the utter opposite of that. Standing straight,

holding a glass out by the base, smiling,

waiting to be thanked,

oh it's a special look I get alright.

They pause, pull their whole heads back, blink.

They look again at the glass, then at me.

Sometimes a small smile melts off the mouth,

like a line of butter off a pat.

I'm so dumb it makes them glad.

They see I actually must be fit for this job;

as they for theirs, me for mine.

What a relief that is for them to know.

It is a relief I am able to provide.

Across the bar, at a lavish event at, say, MoMA

for BlackRock or BridgeCreek or Waterstone

(or perhaps Blackrockwaterstonebridgecreek),

a Voltron of all their hedgings, I dilate

in their eyes into just the kind of kind

but wayward soul they once puked

at tailgates with during their Prince Hal years.

It's nice to see me looking well.

I correct the error. They say, "Thank you,

my man" or "Thank you, my brother,"

or "Thank you, sir." And they should thank me,

thank me for doing my job, for sending them away

confirmed in their world view.

Because I am lucky for them,

people like me. They have created a job.

A job for me. A job for you. A real job

that a poet can almost do, and still be a poet.

$25–$28 an hour to pour wine. Beat that!

I can't. So I don't. Years go by. Like that.

—SPRING, 2014

A Jar of Balloons *or* The Uncooked Rice

"PICK THE ACRID COLORS OUT."

— STEVENS

Have you ever had a haircut so bad
you cried? When you open the drawer
after having poured yourself a bowl of cereal
do you reach for a small or a large
spoon? How conscious are you of your
posture? Will you agree to let a lover use
your toothbrush? Which chemicals'
smells do you like? During which phase
of life did you acquire the bulk of your
friends? Have you ever quit a bad job
emphatically, ripped off a uniform or apron,

thrown the balled-up cloth at a superior,
then stomped off? Grey or gray? Who
most often terminates your telephone
conversations, you or the person to whom
you've been speaking? In your bad dreams
do you ever throw the slow motion
punch? Are you punctual? Is your signature
legible? Have you ever had a birthday go
uncelebrated? What's the largest TV set
you've ever lived with? Showers or baths?
How much cash do you like to carry?
Ever been knocked unconscious?
One large winter coat or layers? If you cross
paths with someone walking a dog, do you talk
first to the person or the dog? Do you eat
or give away pickles? What's the highest
floor on which you've ever lived?
Who is your most promiscuous friend?
Do you get jittery during airplane
turbulence? How jittery? Do you still drink
glasses of milk? How many people
have lived with you? How's your balance?
Have you ever ridden in a limousine?
What are the chances, would you say,
of you becoming, one day, the president
of anything? Greater than none?

When did you learn to write checks?
Can you accurately size up the square
footage in a room? What games do you play
with small children you meet (such as
faking snatching off their noses by poking
a thumb between fingers)? Where you live
is the night sky starry? How high
can you kick? Have you wasted
much thought as to what you'd do
were money suddenly no limitation?
Cake cones or sugar cones? Are you quick
with your wit or do comebacks tend
always to arrive hours later?
Do you keep your photos in albums or
shoeboxes? Are you handy? Do you
cross the street to avoid groups of young men
at night? Have you ever been a part
of one of these groups and watched others
cross streets as a result of you? Do you
match and ball socks or just dump them,
en masse, into the drawer? Do you
bisect your sevens with one of those
squiggly hyphens? Have you gravitated,
traditionally, toward the top or the bottom
bunk? Is it your tendency to order
the same dish over and over, or mix it up?

Are you easy or hard to shop with?
Is your bed up against a wall, or does it sit
in the center of a room, accessible
from both sides? Do you own any pieces
of monogrammed attire? Aisle or window
seat? When eating out, do you set
your knife atop your plate and change
hands? What's your favorite cuss word?
How long did you call your parents' home
your home? How are you at keeping track
of which acquaintances you've told which
thing that's happened to you?
Do you recycle? Do you think that
every bic lighter you see, when in the hands
of a friend, likely once belonged to you?
How are you at not losing pens? Do you
ever pass off profound-sounding statements
of your own creation as famous quotes?
Are you good at putting together kits?
When a friend begins telling a story
he's already told you, do you let him go,
or let him know? When making a shooting-
yourself gesture, do you do the gun barrel
with two fingers or one? Do you insert
the finger-gun into your mouth or press it
to your temple? Do you cut up plastic six-

pack can holders so as to save fish? What
colors have you painted rooms? When
driving by cows do you give into the urge
to moo? What is the most valuable (to you)
possession you've ever lost or had stolen?
Do you miss it? Would you often rather
just stay in the car? Do you always know
the day of the week? Are you ashamed,
like admitting you don't read the newspaper,
when you're way off mark (though, in truth,
the most you can be off is two days?)
What about dates? Do you find you have to ask
aloud every time you're at the bank
or when you're on the grocery store floor,
attempting to pick out milk?
Isn't it nice how willing people are
to tell you the date? Do you have
any "original" items in your home,
anything with a total production
limited to one? Are you accurate
at guessing people's weights and ages?
Do you take into consideration their
feelings when guessing? Can you fall
asleep on your own at the end of the day,
or do you need "help?" Look at your
fingernails: did you just stretch out all five

fingers, palm out, or did you fold your fingers
down over your inward facing palm?
About what parts of life do you have
anxiety about having anxiety? Do
you have a system when it comes to
pockets, or do you blindly dump in
coins, lighter, iPod, phone, smokes, etc.
then fish around each time? Blue or black
pens? Chunky peanut butter or smooth?
When eating bananas, do you peel them
nude at the outset, or peel as you eat?
Do you tear into wrapped presents or
open them neatly with the spoken intent
to save the paper? Do you currently own
a phone with a cord? AM or FM radio?
In school, did you pack or buy lunch?
Have you ever made a scrapbook? What
famous landmarks have you found
especially disappointing? Which do you
(or would you) find more embarrassing:
crying in public by yourself on a bench
or laughing out loud in public by yourself
on a bench? Would you rather drive
or be driven? Ever just want to spit in
someone's face, though you actually really
like the person? Do you engage strangers

in conversations on airplanes? If no,
it's odd, isn't it, when the time comes
to accept peanut packets or order sodas
and you hear their voices? Ever wished
(if you are right-handed) that you could be
left-handed? Do you measure distance
in miles or minutes? Don't tassels feel nice
against the backs of the hands? Are you
in bed at a similar time each night?
Do you imagine sleep as a kind of rising
(you are a basket being pulled gently up
in a hot air balloon) or as a kind of sinking
(you are a flat stone no longer skipping,
disappearing through layers of lake)? Can
you ice skate? Do you own a bathrobe?
Do you go to movies alone? When eating
out, do you prefer, in general, to face
the crowd or the wall? Are you a person
that has certain items that are unequivocally
yours (a coffee mug, a side of the bed,
a chair, a place at the table)? What names
have you thought to name children? How
many different bathrooms would you say
you use on a given day? Are there bathrooms,
(not your own) that you consider a pleasure
to use, even look forward to using?

Are you shy? Do you save your receipts?
Have you ever made love outdoors?
Before throwing spaghetti into the pot,
do you break the bundle in half? Can you
recall a [bowel movement] that produced
the thought: "wow, this is the biggest and
best [bowel movement] of my life?" What
did you call bowel movements as a child?
How old were you when you learned
to read? Do you nap? Isn't stretching
something you always feel you should do
more of while you're doing it? Why must
we always draw a blank after entering
a record store? What's the strangest non-
food item you swallowed as a kid? Do you
use Post-it Notes? Are they still there,
those ascending horizontal lines that marked
your growth as a child up a wall or a door?
In how many cities and towns do you know
your way around? Can you describe
your most frequent freak-out fantasy, or
do the particulars of your situations vary
so that it's always a new table you're
overturning or bus window you're
punching out? Do you ride the bus?
How is your handshake? Can you ever

know for sure if it's too hard or too soft?
When at a museum do you like to walk
around by yourself or take the tour? Can
you recall how the moon looked the first time
you saw it through glasses (if you wear glasses)?
When cooking, do you eyeball or measure?
Do you buy low-fat products? In which
of these opposing clichés ("absence makes
the heart grow fonder" or "out of sight
out of mind") do you find more truth?
Do you go, each time, to the same barber
or hair-stylist? When at the barber or
hair-stylist, do you tend to talk about hair
or realize that people there must always talk
about hair? Was your Christmas tree
(if you had one as a child) fake or real?
What was it topped with? Have you ever
purchased an item with the secret intent
to return it? In which of your pockets
do you carry your wallet? Were you breast
or bottle fed? Can you write at all
with your opposite hand? Do audiences
affect your attempts to urinate
or parallel park? Do you rise to occasions
generally? Butter or margarine?
Do you bookmark or dog-ear your books?

How do you show love to what is yours,
by wearing it in or attempting
to keep it pristine? Do you not mind
fighting losing battles? When was
the last time you wrote a hand-written
letter that was not a greeting card?
Have you ever collected unemployment?
Do you check the dates on coins?
Did you play sports? If so, what
was your number? Were you a planned
or unplanned pregnancy? Do you save
hangers from dry cleaners, amazed
that they're free? When pondering
what things are free, do you always
find yourself inhaling deeply through your nose,
newly aware that air is free?
So much air and all free! What actor(s)
could play you? Are you a fast dresser?
Do you like to be the one that holds
the tickets (for airplanes, movies, etc.)?
Do you trust others? What about
doctors? What is the worst ailment
you've ever been diagnosed with?
Have you ever been diagnosed
as something? How are you
at metabolizing shame? Where,

in your calendar year, have the birthdays
you celebrate tended to cluster?
April? If you went to church as a kid,
did you and your family sit
in the front or in the back?
What things have you been doing
when you've received news that a loved one
has passed on? Can you sleep
with socks on? Can people place
your place of birth by hearing your
accent? What would you try to save
in a fire? Do you wear non-winter hats?
Pulpy or pulp-less orange juice? Do you
always watch for the longest day
of the year and then miss it? Do you
miss lots of things you mean to see
or do? Events you meant to attend?
Picnics involving babies? Do you even
notice? Do you go to the gym?
What is your favorite kind of nut?
Do you remove shoes upon entering?
If no, are you annoyed when you walk
into someone else's home and find
a pile of shoes and a note? Does
walking on rattling street vents make you
anxious? Do you tell people when

you're ticked at them? How are you
at judging clouds of the metaphorical variety
at discerning those which will blow
over and those which will grow to take over
your sky? Is there anyone who likes washing
silverware? What celebrities have you met?
What is your method for dealing with coins?
Spend as you go? Hoard? Roll? Are you
a sucker for foreign accents? Do you
rearrange your furniture regularly? Do you
live in a place where furniture can
be rearranged, or is there really only one
logical place for everything? What gift or
gifts did you receive upon graduating
high school? Do you get mad when a drink
is handed across a bar to you with too much
ice? Mad enough to send it back? Do you
send meals back in restaurants or just
suffer through them? Are there multiple
languages in which you're fluent? Why
did you leave your hometown, if you did?
What are you usually doing when it
occurs to you to clip your toenails?
Can you drive stick? If not, do you
feel that this makes you inadequate?
How do you occupy your time when

in a waiting room or on a train? Books,
magazines, music, or just looking at people
then looking away? Ever French-kissed
the inside of your elbow? Do you live
in a place where tourists come? Are you
skilled at giving directions? Do you
own a record player? If so, have you
owned one all along? What celebrities
do people insist that you look just like?
Is the resemblance such that, when you hear
"You know who you look just like?" and see
the person's finger begin to wag, you can
supply the name or names yourself? Do
you supply the name or names yourself,
or give the person the pleasure of recognition?
Is your name such that it is frequently
mispronounced? Do you attempt to pronounce
foreign words correctly, such as calling
a crescent-shaped roll a cwaSAHN?
Do you like being an American (if you are one)?
Have you ever walked around carrying
a bouquet of flowers just because you like
the looks folks give you on the street?
Are you accurate in determining the ages
of children? What age do you consider
old? How has it changed? Ever just want

to yank the gun from a cop's holster?
Are you a good tipper? When receiving
bad service, are you inclined to think
("it happens") that the server is just having
an off day? Can you spell (without
looking it up) the word "hors d'oeuvre?"
Will you wait for a booth when a table
is available? Will you step out of a shower
to pee? When writing the number 2
do you loop the bottom? Surely at some point
you've worn the clothing of the opposite
sex? Have you ever lived in a room
lit by a bare light bulb? If yes,
when you opened the door and tugged
that jump-back-upping beaded chain and
saw the items of your life in that dimness
did you find it gloriously romantic
or hilariously gloomy? If you don't live alone,
is it you or someone else who changes
light-bulbs? Are you a good speller?
What physical skills have you lost?
Can you still touch your toes? As a child
were you able to turn a cartwheel?
Are you hard on people? What is
the deepest water in which you've been
swimming? You root privately for loose plastic

drink lids, wind-blown and cart-wheeling,

to stay up, to keep rolling and rolling,

don't you? Do you think grades in school

mattered? Can you identify flowers?

Can you identify artists by looking at paintings?

Do you eat the crusts of pizza, or only

when they're excellent or you're hungry?

Do you eat other people's crusts?

Do you cut the crusts off bread?

Are you a member anywhere,

of anything, as of a group of people

that meets at a certain time

and at a certain place? What do you

think about Communism? Can cans

of whipped cream last long in your fridge?

How is your self-control? How is

your cholesterol? Have you ever

spent a night in jail or been

in a physical altercation as an adult? Have

you been cheated on? How

did you handle it? If you could walk

on stage as the lead singer of any band

(in any time period) who would it be?

When no one is looking, will you stick

chewed gum to a chair or table bottom?

When no one is looking, will you do

really just about anything? What is
the most money you've ever found
on a sidewalk or a street? Can you a tie
a tie? What about a bowtie? In which
stores have you ever imagined having
shopping sprees? How are you at Trivial
Pursuit? Crossword puzzles? Does making
a good list ever feel like an accomplishment
in and of itself? Do you clip coupons
or mail in rebates? What's your theory
on why the martini
glass is shaped the way it is? Do you like
animals? Do you find it beautiful when
sidewalks begin to freckle with rain? Seen
from a high window, is there anything
more lovely than when all at once umbrellas
blackly bloom? About what subject (other
than yourself) do you possess the most
knowledge? Do you say caddy-corner or
kitty-corner? Isn't it nice when a drinking
fountain is cold and with the right pressure,
when you push the metal button down
and up pipes a sweet cold glassy little arc
of water? Have you ever been on fire?
Your cuff or your hair? What is the worst
you've ever burned yourself? Can you sing?

Do you find you begin singing
along to songs you know always a bar or so
too early? About what things do you think
you're a snob? Which is snobbier,
ballet or opera? Poetry or croquet?
How about football, beer, and buffalo wings
as a little group? How about cigarettes
and cities and streetlights and walking away
in a leather jacket? Do you use raincoats
or umbrellas? Are your faucets tricky
to the point where if an out-of-towner
were to use your shower, you'd feel the need
to give a tutorial? Are they trickle-y?
When dealing with a knot, are you more likely
to pass the knot to another, sigh and say,
"Can you get this?" or to take the knot
from another and say, "I can get this?"
Are you a take-charge type of person
Are you good with jars? Have you ever
thrown away a crusted pan as opposed
to cleaning it? What is the most difficult
phone call you've ever had to make?
What is the most difficult test you've
ever taken? Do you prefer aiming
fans directly at your face or setting them on
oscillate so as to best relish that all-too-brief

rush of coolness? And when a fan turns away
to, say, rustle an unpaid bill on the end-table,
do you follow it with your face as far as you
can? Do you sit and patiently wait? How
important is it for you to have things to look
forward to? When did you cave in
and buy a cell phone? Do you mind
getting shots or having blood taken?
How many people have you called
your best friend? Do the number of beaches
you've been on exceed your fingers? Does
a sense of true self-worth feel like the light
from a lighthouse, a sudden enveloping
golden feeling that soon moves on, too fast
to chase? Who is your wealthiest relative?
Who is your poorest? Do you ever snort
when you laugh? How are you at building
fires? How about changing flat tires?
Till what age do you hope to live?
Have you found this has changed with time?
When eating Asian cuisine do you ask
for a fork? Do you bite or clip your nails?
Have you ever bitten someone with the goal
being to break skin? Did you like high school?
When walking or driving with a companion
in a place where your companion is familiar

and you are not, do you tend to pay
no attention whatsoever? Were you cruel
or the object of cruelty as a child? The object
of cruelty, right? Aren't children awful?
What's the longest you've ever slept
(not counting when you were sick)?
Is your skin sensitive? Do you set down
sheets of toilet paper before sitting down
on public toilets? Have you ever carved
initials into wet cement? What about
thrown a grocery cart or brick off of a bridge?
At what age (or ages) do you feel
that you were at your stupidest,
by which I mean proudest? Do you
make it a point to go somewhere to watch
fireworks? Are there certain blocks
you avoid because of memories? What is
the oldest object (man-made) you've ever
held? Biggest vehicle you've ever driven?
Does your alarm clock wake you with noise
or radio? Can you think of a particular mirror
in which you appear particularly ugly
or particularly attractive? Do you find
that whatever season is next (Spring,
Winter, Fall, Summer) sounds pretty
good? In which season have

the majority of your memories clustered?
Do you tend (or did you tend) to date
people older or younger than yourself?
Are you thrown when the time changes?
Are you close with anyone bi-polar?
Are you bothered by insects? Have you
noticed how, when the subject is bugs,
the size of the bug will keep increasing?
Have you ever participated in a parade?
Which of the earth's creatures would you
least like to see granted a set of wings?
An alligator? A shark? A snake? Which
of the earth's creatures would you most
like to see granted a set of wings?
Would you nominate the turtle?
Are you ever, while eating something
messy, able to look down your face
and actually see the food particles on it?
Was farting an acceptable activity in your
household? Were you tall, short, or medium
as a kid? Did you go thru phases (tie-
dyed T-shirts and reggae music, then
goth, then jock, say), or have you been
mostly the same over the course of your
life? At what age did you reach your
present height? Do you own a washing

machine and dryer? Do you believe (or
have you ever believed) in heaven? What
technique do you most commonly use
when striking a match? Are you skilled
at eating crabs and lobsters? How are you
with the metric system, or, if that's your
system, with the English system? Which magazines
do you buy? Which do you read standing up
in drugstore aisles? What's your favorite color
of popsicle? When encountering a huge
and many-roomed house, do you ever want
just to find a remote room in its upstairs
and hide? What would you do in there?
Regardless, why is there so much delight
in the thought that whole days might pass
before you were found? Have you ever
had a load of laundry ruined by a pen?
Have you ever run out of gas? Have
you ever been the victim of a burglary?
Do you think you could mug someone?
Do you think you could kill someone
if it came to that? What type of food
have you eaten the most of, would you guess?
Pizza? Chicken? Close your eyes: how many
living-rooms have you memorized? Could
you please call to mind at least

two or three and hold them a moment?
Can you flip your eyelids inside out?
What was your best Halloween costume?
When you imagine your own funeral
does the thought of certain acquaintances
in the same room worry you? Have
you ever picked up a hitchhiker?
Have you ever been a hitchhiker?
How much stock do you put in
the Zodiac? Are your earlobes attached?
Can you recall the first time you saw
snow, or was it something you were
born into, a blurry awareness that snow
was a feature of this world you lived in?
If you didn't grow up with snow,
did you first feel it or see it out a window?
Can you recall the last time the number
of candles on your birthday cake equaled
the number of years you'd been alive?
Could you, right now, name the location
of your social security card? Can you read
music? Do you give in when people
plead? Why isn't it a law that the street
address of every house and building be
clearly marked and in an identical place,
such as is the license plate on a car? Big

weddings or a few friends waiting

on the courthouse steps? What percentage

of your life would you say you spend

alone and recollecting? Okay, you have

a plate of cake and ice cream: Do you go

with a spoon, with a fork, or with both?

Do you have all your original adult teeth?

When you enter a bathroom and find

urine in the toilet, are you inclined to flush

before you use it yourself? Does it depend

upon whether you know the person who

left it, upon the yellowness of the substance?

Do you find it's always green suckers

that disappoint with their flavor,

mint or sour apple when you want lime?

Do you have any racist relatives? What

advice do you generally give to people

who have colds? Are you intrigued by the

lives of movie stars? Are you one of these

people that's always interested in match-

making? Do you like horror flicks? What

tools do you own? Do you sometimes sing

the alphabet song to remember the ordering

of letters? Did you ever think "El-em-en-o-pee"

was itself a letter? What lengths will you

go to to avoid hearing the sound of

your own voice? How many telephone
numbers have you had in your life?
How many addresses? Do you sneeze
thru your nose or your mouth? Do you
sleep on your back, side, or stomach?
Coke or Diet Coke? Do you own,
currently, any furniture you've found
on the street? What items have you stolen?
Cats or dogs? Do you have allergies?
How ripe a banana can you handle?
Have you ever seriously done the limbo?
Have you ever cracked a vase and then tried
to hide the crack by rotating it to face
the wall? Did your parents get angry,
or take it in stride when you broke things
as a child? When replacing toilet paper
do you orient it so that sheets issue from
the bottom or the top of the roll? Can
you draw well? Do you prefer whole, 2%,
or skim milk? Soy? What bones have you
broken? Have you ever pressed your
forearms against the jambs of a door so
that upon stepping out your arms suddenly
rise? Can you give an example of the kind
of lies you tell? Do you litter? Do you ever
drop refuse on the sidewalk and then

ten steps later, turn around, walk back
and properly dispose of it? Do you throw away
Hamburger Helper, Rice-a-Roni , et al.
boxes too early, then have to dig them out
to check the instructions? Have you given
much thought as to what you would eat
for your last meal? Have you ever heard
sex thru a motel room wall? Have you ever
in a motel moaned loudly and shaken a bed
to freak the people out next door? What,
if so, was the silence like afterwards?
Which newspaper sections do you like?
Do you prefer wide-ruled or college-ruled
notebooks? Do you like holding hands
in public with a love? Do you feel bad,
sweat palmed, letting go, like you've just
let the person down by letting go
of his or her hand? Do you like the ways lovers
communicate? How are you at holding
urine? How old is the oldest article
of clothing that's still in your rotation?
Do you own any complete sets
(of dining room chairs, for instance, or figurines
or commemorative plates)? Have you been
eager to complete these, or to keep
these sets intact? And why is there such

satisfaction in any complete set?
Is it because the tendency of all things
and people is to drift, to end up apart,
scattered all over the place,
like a bouquet of helium balloons,
released into the sky that comes down
in little balloon bits in places so far
apart, it actually becomes something,
something to relish and be impressed by,
seeing how far it is they've managed
to drift. What is this called? Entropy?
Do you ever ask aloud the name
of what something is, even when you know?
Does your possession of uncommon
knowledge make you proud or ashamed?
When did you cease calling your mother
"Mommy?" In grade school, did you
raise your hand a lot? Did it snap up
almost against your control, or did you
look around first, and then raise it slowly,
like a periscope peeking out of water?
What is the longest you've ever continuously
driven? What's the longest you've ever continuously
wept? Do you save plastic drugstore bags,
margarine containers, coffee cans, bottles?
While showering has it ever occurred to you

that you wash the parts of your body in
the same order each time? When you stir,
with a spoon, milk or sugar into coffee or
tea, do you like to turn the spoon against
the direction of the swirl? Do you ever ask
someone a question only in hopes that
it will be asked back? Are you then
frustrated if that doesn't work, and the talk
leaps ahead to a new topic? Have you ever
carried a weapon? Have you ever known
a suicide? Do you often feel like slapping
door-opening or elevator-holding strangers
who say, "You're welcome" before you can
thank them? What is the costliest item
you've ever purposefully smashed? Have
you ever inflicted physical pain (even as
simple as a deep thigh pinch) to escape pain
of an emotional sort? It worked,
didn't it? Have you ever won an award?
Have you ever received a loud ovation
in a public place after dropping something?
Do you tend to finish meals in restaurants
or take half home in doggy bags? Should you
be embarrassed that the only flowers you can
identify by sight were those found in your
mother's yard? How many of Shakespeare's

37 plays can you name? Which wrist
do you wear your watch on? Do you sing
karaoke, and, if so, what's your go-to
song? What was your first remembered
movie? Do you eat the cereal that falls
out of the bag and into the bottom of the
box? What about food that falls to the floor?
How large are your feet? Are they,
big or small for your body? Which
brought you more satisfaction—when adults
told you you looked like your mother
or your father? What is your favorite type
of candy? What is your favorite shape
of pasta? What is the fastest you've ever
traveled in a car? After washing hands
in a public restroom, does touching the door-
knob bother you? Will you ever grab
the knob with a paper towel, if only so as
to prolong the period of cleanliness?
What was the first thing you ever wanted
to be when you grew up? How high are your
ceilings? Does the thought that in a few years
phonebooks will no longer fill desk
drawers or sit on the tops of refrigerators
make you slightly sad? How tall are you?
How tall is the tallest person you know?

Ever wished this person could stand
beside the shortest person you know? Would
you agree that a ninety-year-old person
today is significantly "older" than a ninety-
year-old person two hundred years ago,
just in terms of all that person's seen?
Could you describe your wall hangings?
Do you like or dislike having your picture
taken? What color is your hair or was
your hair or would your hair be if you didn't
color it? Could you accurately say, right now,
the thread-count of your bed-sheets?
How old were you when you first flew
in a plane? Who was your favorite
nightly news anchorman (Brokaw, Rather,
Jennings)? Did you have a difficult time
telling them apart when you were young?
Should you just go ahead and say how
old you are? How are you at impersonations?
Do you stick with them when they aren't
going well, or jump ship? One CD at a time,
over and over, or always a mix? Do you look
forward to your birthday? At what age
did you cease looking forward to your
birthday? Were your parents younger or
older than most of the parents of your

peers? Did you lose your virginity to a
virgin? Which board games do you
own? What's your favorite? What music
did you like when you were thirteen?
Do you have siblings? If Caucasian do you tan
or burn? Can you recall a place that's
prompted you to say, "this is, without doubt,
the prettiest place I've ever been?" Is
there anything you can't do that most
people can (swim, ride a bicycle, drive,
snap your fingers, whistle, wink?)
How are you at naming a dog's breed?
What name have you always thought
would also be fitting for you? What name
would you have if you were of the opposite
sex? Do you like dancing enough to go
out dancing? Is your handwriting small
or large? Is it your nature to give advice?
Do you ever take another's story and make
yourself the protagonist in its retelling?
When, while conversing, a fleck of spittle
flies out of someone's mouth and lands
on your face, is your tendency to pretend
it didn't happen, make a display, or
subtly (after a pause) wipe it away? How
many ex-loves are you currently in

contact with? Have you ever done hard
drugs? How competitive are you? Do
you attempt to refold clothes in stores
after having tried them on? If no,
is your reasoning that to fold and restock
is somebody's job and why should
you help her with her job when she
doesn't help you with yours? What
do you do about indefinite pronouns?
"He," "she, " or the nearly impossible
to maintain "he/she"? Do you find
you always exaggerate, at least a little,
how little you've slept the prior night?
At what point do you round down to zero?
Are you able to sleep well on buses,
airplanes, backseats of cars? Do you get
frightened when your hands, legs, etc.
fall asleep? "Oh" or "O"? Do you go
to the doc when sick or try to tough it out?
Do you have health insurance?
Have you ever disappeared on someone?
At what age were you heaviest? Do you
correct people's small errors in pronunciation
by, to their unspoken embarrassment,
correctly pronouncing the word in question
in the next sentence? Do you completely

remove pull tabs from pop cans? Do you call
soda "soda" or "pop?" What movies
haven't you seen that most people have?
Any piercings you want to talk about?
Have you ever been kicked out of
school? If someone swung open
your refrigerator, would they find food,
wonderful food and juices and fresh milk,
or just condiments? Do you bring along
a pillow when you travel? Do your friends
know one another? Do you have any friends
with whom you've never had what you'd
consider a "deep" conversation? If so,
do you consider this a bad thing or just
a thing? In winter (if such applies)
do you remove window air conditioners?
Ever licked a sucker down to its paper
stick? Ever even tried? What do you use
to wipe yourself when out of toilet paper?
What is the most recent story you find
yourself telling people over and over?
Do you secretly miss sleepovers?
If a band or brand becomes too popular,
do you cease to like it? Which do you prefer:
keeping secrets or telling everyone?
Have you ever had surgery? How many

people from high school do you keep in
touch with? Do you ever swallow your
gum? Were you skilled at climbing trees?
Have you ever fallen out of a tree?
What is the highest height you've fallen from?
What about figuratively? Do you plan to be
buried or cremated? Have you ever sat
down at a table and everyone has gotten
up? Laptop or desktop? Why
is the inclination always to assume
that a street musician possesses talent
and a tragic story if the instrument
he plays is a saxophone? Do you play
the lotto? What's the most money
you've ever given to a homeless person?
What movies have you cried in?
Are you irked when a cashier hands back
over a buck in coins? At what age did age
suddenly seem not to matter so much?
Did you have braces? Front or back
of a canoe? If you could date any celebrity
(including dead celebrities, in their primes)
who would it be? What are the toughest
pieces of mail you've ever had to open
(give top three)? Do you look before
you flush? Do you divide people into

opposing categories (such as "windows-
up" and "windows-down" people)?
Any trophies? Do you travel heavy
or light? What is your opinion of jewelry
on men? What about clothes on dogs?
When you find yourself, say, on a building-
top as dawn whitens and you feel
that unfortunate burst of energy shooting
like bright veins through your fatigue (all
sound-tracked with birdsong's beginnings)
do you find you always want to change
your life? Have you ever sued anyone?
When people are attempting to leave
do you let them go, or do your best
to make them stay? Faces or names?
As a driver, are you aggressive or
defensive? Have you ever fasted? When
naked, are you capable of forgetting
you're naked? Do you ever think,
"Yep, this will make a good rag"?
First job? Worst job? Current job?
Ever had a job where you see face
after face after face (cashier, club
bartender, ticket-taker at a theater,
toll-booth collector), one face after
another, faces like bubbles that appear

and then pop, although occasionally,
as with a bartender, re-appearing
so that a tiny relationship (made up
of a few well-executed gestures) starts up?
Big, little or medium-sized dogs? How
are you at keeping your word? Over
the years have you noticed your voice
has changed? Do you tend to be
praised by dentists? Do you send out
a Christmas letter, filling people in
on your year? Have you ever been lost
in a parking lot? Has anyone ever left
without you? Are you quick to admit
fault, accept blame? Do you have
plants? Do you save room for dessert?
Even when you know there's no food,
do you open the fridge and stare until
the fridge's motor begins to hum? Are
you good about turning out lights? Do
you often enter rooms to get something
and then blank as to why you went in?
Does this frighten you? Are you frightened
by your occasional slumps in memory,
and tell others? Have you ever lied
about your age? What's the largest amount
of years you've tacked on or shaved?

Isn't it miserable when you get home
and have no clue what to do with yourself?
If you plan to be buried, which objects
would you like to share your casket?
Would you enter the earth in casual or
formal attire? Would you enter in
serious or ironic attire? Do you have any
photos of just yourself in frames? Do you live
alone? How many keys are on
your key ring? What do they unlock?
Do you tell people when they bore you?
Have you ever, through a window, seen
a naked neighbor? If so, did the sight
titillate or revolt? Do you smoke
pot? Have you ever worked in a strip
mall? Are you a fast or a slow reader?
What kind of music do or did your folks
like? Can you chant a chant children
chanted when you were a child? At
what age did you know the most good
jokes? Do you write things down
or think, "I think I can remember that?"
Would you rather go first, generally?
Isn't it crazy that at one point
you didn't know what a rose was,
didn't know your name or even how

to blow your nose? About what subject
have you forgotten the most? Have you
more often broken up with significant
others or been broken up with? Do
people tell you you look younger than
you are? Are they right? How do you take
compliments? How do you take
rejection? What is the most unsettling
creature, such as a tarantula, that you've
held or handled? A snake at the zoo?
Do you open people's medicine cabinets?
Do you feel, on the whole, guiltier
when you get caught or don't get caught?
Do you feel guilty about not feeling guilty
enough when you don't get caught?
What are your feelings on reincarnation?
It's not a bad idea, is it? Can you sit
still well? Ever had a job where you
pass people tools? Dental hygienist? Grip?
Are you a good or bad assistant?
Which of your friends had pools?
Have you ever tooted in a bathtub,
(be honest) and bent forward to greet
the rising stink bubble nose-first? Are
you fun? Are you quick to purchase
new technologies? Have you ever

been burned by a video game system
that never caught on? Is your can-opener
electric? What is your opinion of
greeting cards? Would you rather receive
a note on loose-leaf and two bucks, or
do you like the fact someone went,
for you, to a drugstore, and stood there
in the card aisle, opening, opening?
Is there anyone out there who hates you?
Is there anyone out there who hates you
justifiably? Do you care? Do you like
showing others your bruises, cuts,
and scars? Did you ever believe
that pro wrestling wasn't fake? What was
the first "adult" book you recall reading?
Do you like big round numbers?
Do you like to do things (get out of bed,
leave a friend's apartment, make
a difficult phone call) at exact times
("I will get up off this
couch at exactly 11:15 PM.")?
Ever wonder how life was before clocks?
Do you find baseball boring and slow
or do you feel absolutely the opposite?
Have you ever wished your room
could be dusted for fingerprints, as in

the cop movies, just so you could see?
Do you, in general, like to see? Do
you like to open presents early?
When no one is around, do you do
number two with the bathroom door
flung open? Why is this so damned
great? Would you say you "exist,"
in the sense that you can sense some
thread of you-ness tying you together—
as handwriting ties together a person's
hand-written words, the way you behave
in bank lines, around bosses, around
lovers, friends—in all situations?
Doesn't your heart just plummet
when you cause a big mess?
Do you hate the rich? Or pity them?
How much help have you had in life?
How many beds have you had in your life?
As a little kid, did you consciously act
like a little kid? Do you see a shrink?
Have you ever been on a blind date?
Where did your grandparents end up?
Did they stay where they were or
migrate toward the heat, chasing
sunshine like cartoon potted plants that
creep about on tip-toe roots? At

a certain point will we all switch
to "old-people's clothes" or will we
go on dressing as we always have until
we learn what we we've been wearing
ARE old people's clothes? Macs
or PCs? Do you finish most books
you start, or do they lay around on coffee
tables and nightstands, open, face-down,
slowly deforming? Do you take good
care of your things? Have you ever had
an injury from sleeping oddly? Do you
belong to any online friend networks,
or has that box where you're asked
to cram yourself into 200 words always
been too intimidating? Are you very
(or would you be if you let yourself be)
hairy? Where, if you have a choice,
do you like to sit when at the movies,
toward the front or toward the back?
Do you like to turn around and look
at the shining, rapt faces? Do you like
watching people watch tennis,
the uniformly turning faces? When
did you learn to tie shoelaces? Do
you remember when 3 o'clock
was the most important time? Boxers

or briefs (if such applies)? What is
the worst injury you've ever sustained
at a beach? Do you like to go in?
Do you like going around shirtless
or going around in bathing suits,
or are you secretly electric with nerves?
As far as places you've been, if you are
tallying the list for the sheer pleasure
of a large number, do airports count?
Shoes with Velcro: ever owned any?
Who do you think has more friends,
me or you? When indoors and too warm
is your impulse to blame the room
or fear a fever? Is a lack of exterior
corridors how you go about judging
a motel? Have you more often stayed
in hotels or motels? Have you ever walked
along a highway for reasons other than
a broken-down car? Is there any ordinary
walk more desolate than the longer-
than-you'd-think walk between huge
joined chain stores (such as between
a Best Buy and a Home Depot) where you
vacillate as to whether to drive, but don't
because it's all the same parking lot?
Have you ever sharpened a knife?

As a teenager, did you loiter? A lot?
What is the longest you've ever gone
without speaking to another human?
Do you think you could go a week?
To whom have you caused the greatest
joy? Who has hurt you the worst?
When is the last time you purchased
pornography? Do you tend toward
pigeon-toed or penguin-footed?
Did you ever purchase CliffsNotes?
Do people generally listen to you
or ignore you? Are you vigilant about
seatbelts? Do you currently own any
balls? Peppermint or spearmint? Which
do you find increases more rapidly,
your age or your idea of what age is old?
Why does it feel like such a victory,
just remembering certain instances,
certain people? Do you set your watch
at the exact time or ahead? If ahead,
do you find you simply subtract
the difference, thus making the point
of setting your watch ahead entirely
irrelevant? Do you mess with things,
such as a watch's tiny winding knob,
just thumbnail it out, then thumb it in?

Do you ever mess with the button inside
the fridge that makes the light go off
and on, just press it flat a few times?
Does your weight go up and down
or stay the same? What rollercoasters,
generally, is your mental health strapped
into? Have you ever been caught in the act
of sex? Were you secretly proud?
When was the last time you ran
as fast as you possibly could? You can
recall when you've been pooped on
by birds, no? Do you ever find yourself
(particularly when dressed up) tallying
up the total cost of all that you have
on? When naked do you ever think
"zero"? Do you say "take a shower,"
or "have a shower?" Is "like" your vocal
tic or is it "you know?" At what age
did you buy your final pair of cleats?
Does scrawling your name on a screen
when you pay by card scare you?
As if they might think you are a forger?
In what grade in school did people
begin to "date?" Were you in on this?
If you had to dispose of a dead body
how would you do it? Who is your least

judgmental friend? Do you own or
have you ever owned leather pants? Is
there anyone to whom you can tell
everything? Can you sing any songs
a cappella from beginning to end?
Do you like being followed around
a house by an animal and then stopping,
saying, hands on hips, "What are you
looking at, little fellow?" Do you prefer
being the more loved or the more
loving, the hunter or the hind?
How many dogs, alive right now,
do you know by name? What is
the first website you go to after
you check your email? Who,
of those you know personally,
has had the shortest marriage? What
is the oldest couple you know
that has gotten divorced? Aren't
old-age divorces especially sad?
Did you know that Robert Frost
loved gossip, and was secure enough,
as an old man, to admit it?
Do leather belts, when the excess
isn't tucked into a belt loop, confuse you
into thinking they're exposed penises?

Do you then try to sneak back
into that unknowing place, and continue
trying to see them as 2-D penises?
Two piece bathing suits or one
(again, if such applies)? Are you more
of an exhibitionist or a voyeur?
But the sight of yourself having sex
in a mirror is exhilarating, no?
Is there any furniture of your parents'
(a clock, an antique chair, a crystal bowl)
that you've had your eye on
for most of your remembered life?
When you see an old man or woman
in a supporting role at a film's outset,
do you immediately begin thinking,
"Well, it's a given this one is going to die."
Is it really a bad thing that most films
are predictable, as little else
is? Do you, if you celebrate it,
celebrate Christmas on Christmas
or Christmas Eve? When making approximate
sock matches, do you pair based on texture
("these feel about right") color
("well, these two have gold toes") or both?
Did you have chicken pox early in life?
How much do you make? Is it less

now than you've made in the past?
Which dish of your mom's is or was
your favorite? Which was your least favorite?
Do you listen to phone messages
all the way through or delete them?
What is the longest book or series
of books you've ever read? Are you at a loss
when you finish? Are you a sucker
for products on infomercials, adhesive
putties, magnetic brooms, new devices
for rapidly dicing vegetables? What about
the extras, thrown in at the end,
though predictable as a rock band's
big hit delayed until a concert's encore—
("All this for only!")—are you a sucker
for those too? Do you find
it frustrating that, although knowing
how certain things "work" (for instance,
how a love interest not calling you back
automatically increases your interest),
you can't help but being drawn in?
But isn't it human to be drawn in?
But then again, what is it to be "human"
anyway and why do we even want
to be it? Why not something else?
Which would you rather be? A blue whale,

unconscious and in tune? Or God?
Do you ever miss appointments entirely?
Do you ever feel guilty about wanting
too much, and monitor, like a waistline,
your wants? Isn't it nice to stir butter
around in, say, a pot of pasta, and watch
the pat dwindle and dwindle? "Oh, and here
it comes again, now a little smaller,"
—do you think that? Likewise,
do you like watching flying helium balloons
disappear into specks? Do you watch
loved ones disappear on train platforms
or in rearview mirrors? Do you watch
as long as you can? How often is it,
would you say, that your life, to you,
resembles a movie? Less often than before?
Are you adept at remembering birthdays?
As a host, are you skilled and willing,
skilled and unwilling, unskilled and willing,
or unskilled and unwilling? In general,
do you feel it's your fault if someone
is not having a good time? Are you
a person that thinks he can fix people?
Can you? Can you recreate the facial expression
you use when purchasing items like
condoms or Preparation H? Plastic

or paper at the grocery? Are you one
of these people who just doesn't give
a shit? If no, do you think that these
people actually exist? Are they
conscious of the fact that they don't
care and chant their un-caring down
their collars? Do you ever wish you could
break dance, just spin and spin on your
head in a subway station on a pizza
box? Who would you guess is happier,
you or your next door neighbor? Do you like
black licorice? Do you ever invite yourself?
Tonic water or soda water (yellow
label or blue)? What is your favorite
type of apple? Do you buy generic?
What won't you buy generic?
Do you think you're capable of
letting yourself fall without bracing
your body in any way? How much
money would that take? How much
will? How little must you sleep
before you round down to none,
tell others you didn't sleep a wink?
Three hours? Two? One? Do you still
have possessions in someone else's
attic? How conscious are you of your

breath? When eating Thanksgiving dinner
do you like to mash together the turkey
and stuffing with the potatoes and beans,
or keep them apart and eat them separately?
What's been your toughest birthday?
Are their any card games you'd say
you are extremely good at? Can you predict
rain with aches? Do you knock on
wood? Are you famous? In other words
do more people that you haven't met
know who you are than people
you have met? If you opened
the hood of your own smoking car,
would you have any idea what you were
looking at? Do you like to pretend?
How often do you Google yourself?
Do you have any collections of things
(books, wines, sports cards, jeans,
fountain pens, stamps, toy figurines
in original packaging) that you actively
grow? Who is the animal you've loved
the most? What was its name? Kipper?
Munchkin? Jake? Do you like
guessing names? What about guessing
games? At what age was your first
kiss? How often do you think of this?

More than once a year? How often
do you sleep till you wake? Is there
anything better than climbing into bed
and knowing this, knowing you'll be
sleeping an indefinite length? What's
the most you've ever shelled out
for shoes? Do you like to camp?
Have you ever killed an animal with
a car? A gun? Have you ever been in a boat
from which you couldn't see the shore?
What catalogs do you get? Can you
ski? If you could own a pro sports
franchise, which sport would it be?
Which team? Who was your favorite
teacher? Is he/she still where he/she
was, still teaching? What alterations
to your form have you imagined?
Unscrewable limbs? An extendable
neck? A third arm, very short,
projecting from your sternum? Perhaps
four more fingers on each hand
to fill the gaps between fingers, so as
to double the noise you could make
when drumming on tables while waiting,
four more fingers to keep fine things
like sugar from falling through fingers

(though a doubling of fingers would,
of course, double the number of gaps)?
Do you use words between words,
like "spork," or "skort," or "shart,"
finding them legitimate gap-fillers
or would you mock someone you knew
who showed up and said, "Hey, pass me
a spork?" Do you wash your hands
before you eat? In restaurants? What about
before you wash hands? Can you play
guitar? Do you floss? Have you
ever pulled your car to the shoulder
due to driving rain, and then just sat,
waiting, totally overwhelmed? Are you
disappointed by your windshield
wipers' highest speed? Can you talk
like Donald Duck? Are you a fast
walker? Do you or have you ever had
a nickname? Were you one of these
people at whom nicknames, like
noodles at cabinets, were thrown?
Do you count the books you have
by a certain author, or cds you have
by a certain artist, and then just delight
a moment in the number (ah, 13
or ah, 7)? If you smoke, do you stub

butts mid-way, or always suck them
down to the filter's end? Do ringing
phones on televisions cause you
confusion? Do you take your pulse
a lot? Are you ever afraid to take it,
in the way one is afraid to take
a receipt from an ATM? Are you
salaried or paid hourly? At what age
did you cease taking baths, or cease
exclusively taking baths? How rare
or not rare are those days in which
you don't leave your home
or don't spend any money? That
feels great, doesn't it? Who am I?
Have you ever let a roach or some
other bug in your apartment or home
live? Do you always eat
breakfast? Did you cheat in school?
Did you let others cheat off you?
At what age (if such applies)
did the thought of a pink room begin
to sicken you? Were you allowed,
as a child, to watch R-rated movies?
What was your first X-rated movie?
Which minds do you admire? Any?
Have you ever stayed overnight

in a hospital? Do you like being
a patient, and having people coming
to see you, like a king, to kiss the ring
of your sickness, or are you driven
mad that you can't get up, constantly?
Do you hope for a swift abrupt death,
or would you rather spend time
on the deathbed? Have you ever,
imagining the deathbed as a kind
of perfectly edited highlight reel of your life,
filed away certain items to recall later
—such as "yes, that first time I biked
home from work through Times Square
at about 4 am, hopping through red lights,
and no one was there,
and the whole square, that 75 foot tall
cube of light, was something I was
having to myself, and the wet white litter
was everywhere, just an unbelievable amount
yes yes, absolutely, that definitely
makes the deathbed reel?" Would
you put lowlights on your reel?
Say, some childhood scene when you spilled
a whole quart of yogurt on your lap,
or the time you waited in a 45 minute line
on your birthday for a rollercoaster

you ended up too afraid to ride or
when you pushed a friend's little brother
into a swimming pool in his clothes
and their mother screamed, screamed at you
because the child could have died?
And is it not that way already, everything
with its weight and place?
Do you begin to think of yourself
as a year older before your birthday? If so,
how many days or months before? Do
you mind when dogs lick your face?
If not, will you pretty much let any
non-stray dog lick your face? Have
you ever flown first class? Do you ever
fantasize about returning
with your present abilities to a
situation where your lack of those
abilities caused you shame, or even just
ordinariness? Did you attempt
to dominate those younger than you?
What is your favorite
month? Are there businesses that you
boycott? Were you a real go-getter
when it came to selling raffle tickets?
Raising money? Securing magazine subscriptions?
Among relatives, who is the biggest

low-life? How tall was your dad?
When you sense your breath is bad
do you exhale into your cupped hand
then attempt to sniff with your nose?
The cold showers you've been forced to take
have survived in memory, have they
not? From top to bottom, off
the top of your head, are traffic lights
red-yellow-green or green-yellow-red?
Do you know who knows things like that?
How frequently do you say your
own name followed by "is dead, is
dead" in the imagined voices of
sorrowful friends? Do you find this
weirdly exciting? How many people,
right now, know exactly where
you are? None? Do you like putting things
in order? Do you like putting small edibles,
nuts, and candy corn in your nose?
Do you attempt to describe in detail
your dreams to others? How's your gut?
Are you right about people? About
whom have you been wrong? Regarding
underwear and socks, do you replace
piece by piece, or every two or three
years overhaul the whole drawer?

How much tolerance do you have
for coincidence (at what point, I mean,
will religious thoughts kick in)? Any
authors whose work you've read
every single published word of? Have
you dated multiple people with the same
name and later confused friends when
these same-named exes have come into
your mind and out of your mouth? Have
you ever saved bottle-caps so as to keep
tabs on your drinking? Do you like
finding evidence of things you do,
like movie ticket stubs folded in your wallet
from a movie you saw months ago,
Or perhaps a menu from a friend's wedding
in a suit pocket that causes you
to suddenly remember exactly what you ate
on a day three long years ago? Have you ever
liked an ID photo so much you've kept
the ID or become indignant at the fact
that you had to give it back at the end
of the experience for which it was needed?
Do you generally know what to do?
Somebody you went to grade school with
must die violently: who will it be? Do
you own a radio that's only a radio?

Do you mop floors or scrub on all fours?
Do you like making single tall stacks
such as of Oreos or poker chips? How
distinct from one another are your
days? Are there, for instance, activities
that you only perform on certain days
(for example, when you were a child
on energetic Saturday mornings you might have
watched cartoons then played baseball,
or on Sunday mornings might have lugged
a newspaper big as a log into the house or gone
to church—did you go to church and do
the whole "stand up/sit down/stand up/sit
down" thing—then later had the stiffest,
more formal dinner of the week as anxieties
like cloud icons in weather reports—homework,
a bully, a huge crush—reappeared
to smudge your bright ideas of tomorrow)
that give to each day of the week
a character that although woven together
of too many factors for a source to be
fingered, is nonetheless there, existent,
a certain "Sunday-ness" or "Saturday-ness"
(or somewhat blander "Wednesday-ness")
that reveals itself in comments such as
"I know it's a Tuesday but all day it's felt

like a Thursday" or "This Sunday really
feels like a Sunday?" In other words,
do you have a routine? Do you like this
routine or non-routine? Do you think
you could be happy without one, with
a routine of having a non-routine?
How long does it take you to learn
a grocery store? Have you ever been
to Africa or Asia? Isn't it an odd feeling,
to see a building or a house that you've
never seen, despite having passed by it
literally hundreds of times? How does this
make you feel? That because a simple act
such as fitting your key into your door
(and jiggling it with the necessary jiggle)
does not add to, but rather disappears
like a thief into a crowd of thieves into
the hundreds of times you've performed
this identical act, that you can't help keep
missing something? And what is that thing?
How important is it that you find it?
Do you scale from 1 to 10? How many times
have you seen It's A Wonderful Life
roughly? Do you ever have the desire
to organize your experiences by, say,
photographing every bed in every hotel you've

ever slept in or every cluttered coffee table
you've spent a talk-filled night around
or every bar-stool you've sat on long enough
to warm it? What would this accomplish,
this endless compiling? Would it matter
that there'd never be time to sort through
the stacks, or is the important thing simply
that the stacks be there, to be tipped over,
then righted and squared with soft, short,
parallel-palmed pushes? At which fast
food establishment (other than McDonald's)
have you had the most meals? Ever
been skinny dipping? Which do you think
is more infectious, a whisper or a yawn?
Which do you think is more irresistible,
a window or a mirror? What about a piano
in a room with a dusty shaft of sunlight
and no one to forbid you? But isn't it a shame,
isn't it actually a tragedy that the bulk of life,
save for the occasional plaqued fish,
once caught, noticed, must be thrown
back in? How old were you when you first
felt the need for a filing cabinet? Pine
or lemon-scented cleaning solutions?
Are you a believer in holistic medicine?
Are you a believer in just about everything?

Have you ever ridden a motorcycle?
Do you dream about having your
problems' opposites? An apartment
so large you feel lost, small?
The one that won't pick up her phone
ever, driving you mad, burning your
cheek with her chatter? Why is there
pleasure in pressing a piano key so
softly there is no sound? Generally,
do you try to solve problems by
embracing them or eradicating them?
Do you think this should wind down?
Any memorable sunsets you'd like
to throw in? Or is there no need
to remember sunsets because today's
is or was or will be orange enough,
and with the right mellowness? Any friends
named Andy? Any Bobs? What is your
expression for preparing to make
an exit? Folding up shop? Breaking down?
Which questions will you remember? Which
will you mention? Are you ticklish?
Will you forgive me (if you feel the need)
for this mess? When someone
apologizes, are you quick to accept?

ACKNOWLEDGMENTS

"A Big Ball of Foil in a Small NY Apartment" appeared in *NY Quarterly* and *Best American Poetry 2005*.

"Tap Water" appeared in *Sixth Finch*.

"Sleep, Mothers" appeared in *Super Machine* and *At Length*.

"A Jar of Balloons or The Uncooked Rice" appeared in *Sixth Finch* and *Best American Poetry 2010*.

Many thanks to all the editors, series editors, and guest editors.

NOTES & THANKS

My first and deepest debt is to my parents, Bob and Joanne Yeager, who gave me the reins to my own life fairly early and have been hoping and praying ever since. Your love has been my bedrock.

Thank you to my amazing wife, Chelsea Whitton, daily evidence that I am the luckiest man in New York.

I owe much to the patience and passion of so many great writing teachers; they are, in order of their arrival into my life, Paula Knight, James Downie, Paul Hendricks, Michael Marchal, Greg Hrbek, Dan Barden, Hilene Flanzbaum, Fran Quinn, Susan Neville, Glyn Maxwell, Fanny Howe, Robert Polito, and David Lehman.

To my friends, poet and non-poet alike, please forgive my absences, and accept my gratitude for the inspiration over the years: Malachi Black, my brother in the art and stay against confusion, Cate Marvin, Jeff Smith, Jade Sharma, Jack Kukoda, Brad Christopher Hisey, Corky Steiner, Jerry Rippey, the entire Shiels Family, the Bacha and Yeager extended families, Bob, Danneal, and Lindsay Whitton, Eric Sullivan, Laura Cronk, Megin Jimenez, Terrance Hayes, PJ Moriarty, Justin Marks,

John Deming, Sean Logan, Ido Ben Smuel, Jean Michel Alperin, Julianne Hide, Marcus Wise, Elizabeth Koch, Alex Seal, Nick Adamski, Stephanie Berger, Eric Conroe, Mateusz Broughton.

Thank you as well to the KGB Monday Night Poetry community and all the poets I've had the great fortune to introduce. Thank you to the MacDowell Colony, where "Sleep, Mothers" was mostly written, and to the wonderful artists I've come to know through my experiences there. Thank you to the Pinch Food Design community, who perhaps know me better than any other, and my workshop gang: Mark Gurarie, Alex Crowley, Ali Power, Katie Byrum, Keara Driscoll, Lily Goderstad, Jess Smith.

Thank you to Eric Appleby and all at Forklift Books. Special thanks to Matt Hart, not only for helping to select and edit these poems, but for the idea of "a book of five or six long poems; and that's it."

Greatest, deepest, highest thanks and praise to God, Ens, the Unbegotten Good, call it what you will, and to the Jesuits at St. Xavier high school many years ago, who pointed me to the one whose vision has become dearest to me among all others: Paul Tillich. No road inward isn't rocky; one can only hope to be well-shod.

"Tap Water" is dedicated to Patrick and Carrie Shiels. Given its length and conclusion, it was, in hindsight, probably not the best choice to read at their wedding, but their wedding was the occasion that brought it into its final shape.

"Red Wine or White Wine" is for Steve Hamm and Zack Griffits.

"Poem [You're Henry Hudson]" is an imaginative / speculative poem as much at it is an historical poem. Events deviate slightly from recorded accounts of the mutinied explorer's last days at sea. Hudson's personality in the poem is entirely the author's own creation.

ABOUT THE AUTHOR

Matthew Yeager's poems have appeared in *Sixth Finch, Gulf Coast, Minnesota Review, Bat City Review,* and elsewhere, as well as *Best American Poetry 2005* and *Best American Poetry 2010.* His short film "A Big Ball of Foil in a Small NY Apartment" was an official selection at eleven film festivals in 2009-2010, picking up three awards. Other distinctions include the Barthelme Prize in short prose and two MacDowell fellowships. The co-curator of the long running KGB Monday Night Poetry Series, he has worked in the NY catering industry for thirteen years in various capacities: truck driver, waiter, sanitation helper, sanitation captain, floor captain, bartender, bar captain, service instructor, and lead captain.